An Introduction to
British Mammals

A Photographic Guide

Liz Gogerly

WAYLAND

This book is a differentiated text version of
The Wayland Book of Common British Mammals by Shirley Thompson

First published in Great Britain in 2009 by Wayland, a division of Hachette Children's Books

Wayland
338 Euston Road,
London NW1 3BH

Copyright © Wayland 2009

All rights reserved.

Editor: Julia Adams
Designer: Ruth Cowan
Picture researcher: Shelley Noronha

Cover photograph: A badger. Title page: a stoat climbing down a tree. This page (from top): A rabbit eating plums; a red squirrel; a bank vole eating a hazelnut; a common seal resting on some rocks. Contents page (from top): A wood mouse; a noctule bat; some roe deer; a domestic cat.

Picture credits
Bruce Coleman Collection 9 bottom (Jane Burton), 12 (Jens Rydell), 19 bottom (Jane Burton),27 (Hans Reinhard), 28 bottom (Hans Reinhard); **FLPA** 1 (R Tidman), 19 top (R Wilmshurst), 23 bottom (R P Lawrence), 28 top (R Tidman), 29 (D A Robinson), 41 top (Michael Callan), 45 (Foto Natura); **Papilio Photographic** 4 top (Neil Miller), 5 (Robert Pickett), 6 (Jamie Harron), 7 (William Dunn), 8 (Steve Austin), 10 bottom (Steve Austin), 10 top (Alastair Shay), 11 (Alastair Shay), 13 (Alastair Shay), 14 (William Middleton), 15 (Michael Maconachie), 16 (Robert Pickett), 17 (Laura Sivell), 18 (Steve Austin), 20 (Mike Buxton), 21 (Chris Beddall), 22 (Ken Wilson), 23 top (Chris Beddall), 26 (Clive Druett), 30 (Robert Pickett), 31 (David Smith), 33 (Alastair Shay), 34 (Brian Knox), 35 left (Annie Poole), 35 right (David Smith), 36 (Clive Druett), 37 top (Jane Sweeney), 38 top (Ken Wilson), 39 top (Clive Druett), 39 bottom (Robert Gill), 40 right (Clive Druett), 41 bottom (Robert Pickett), 46 (Clive Druett); **Touchstone Images** 4 bottom, 40 left; **University of Aberdeen** 24 (Ben Wilson); **Wayland Picture Library** 37 bottom; **Zefa** 9 top, 25; **iStock** *front cover* (Chris Crafter), 32 (Chris Crafter), 38 bottom (Filip Fuxa). All maps, and artwork on page 42 by Victoria Webb. Artwork on pages 43, 44 and 45 by Peter Bull.

British Library Cataloguing in Publication Data
Gogerly, Liz
   An introduction to British mammals
   1. Mammals - Great Britain - Juvenile literature 2. Mammals
   - Great Britain - Identification - Juvenile literature
   I. Title
   599'.0941

ISBN 978 0 7502 5439 7

Printed and bound in China

Wayland is a division of Hachette Chidren's Books, an Hachette Livre UK company

www.hachettelivre.co.uk

Contents

Introduction

◄ *Wood mice have furry coats to keep them warm and dry.*

All the creatures that live in the world belong in an animal group. These groups are mammals, reptiles, amphibians, fish, birds and insects. This book is about mammals. This group includes human beings, dolphins and squirrels. These creatures are all linked in a special way. The mother gives birth to her young. In other animal groups the mother lays eggs. Female mammals also have mammary glands that produce milk. The young mammals feed on milk from their mother.

▼ *A baby Jersey cow drinks milk from its mother.*

There are about 4,500 different species of mammal in the world. Mammals come in all shapes and sizes. However, all mammals have some fur or hair on their bodies. They are also warm-blooded.

▲ The common seal has a layer of fat called blubber to keep warm.

In Britain, there are 64 species of mammals living on the land (land mammals). There are over 20 mammals that live in or visit the seas around Britain (marine mammals). In this book you can find out about some of our most common wild mammals. These include foxes, rabbits, wood mice and bats. Some of these creatures live all over Britain. Others live only in a few parts of the country. You may never see some of these mammals in the wild. These animals are often shy. Many are also nocturnal. This means they mostly come out at night.

At the back of this book (see pages 42–43) there are hints to help you spot different mammals. Each creature leaves its own footprint or track. They also leave behind droppings or leftover food. By following these clues you may be able to discover wild mammals for yourself.

 **Common seals**

Maps
In this book there is a map to show where each mammal lives. The map above shows where common seals are found.
The shaded red area shows where these seals mostly live.

Hedgehog

Latin name: *Erinaceus europaeus*

Habitat: forest, hedgerows, cultivated land, gardens

Body size: 15–30 cm, tail 3 mm

Weight: 1.5–2 kg

Life span: up to 5 years

▲ *Hedgehogs are active at night.*

■ **Hedgehogs**

Hedgehogs are the only mammal with spines living in Britain. Adult hedgehogs can have 5,000 sharp spines. Underneath the spines, hedgehogs have soft fur. When hedgehogs are scared they roll up into a ball. Then they raise their spines to protect themselves. Hedgehogs cannot see very well but they have good senses of smell and hearing.

They eat mainly slugs, snails, earthworms and caterpillars. Most hedgehog babies are born in June. There are usually between three and five babies in a litter. During winter, hedgehogs hibernate in nests of leaves or straw. At this time their heartbeats drop from about 190 to 20 beats per minute.

Mole

Latin name:	*Talpa europaea*
Habitat:	wooded hilly areas
Body size:	14 cm, tail 28 mm
Weight:	100–150 g
Life span:	up to 2.5 years

Moles are common in Britain but you will rarely see one. They spend most of their lives underground. They dig networks of tunnels with their spade-like front feet. They push the loosened soil to the top of each tunnel. These piles of earth are called molehills. Many people think moles are a pest because molehills ruin their gardens.

Moles have soft, silver-black fur. Their tiny eyes are the size of pinheads. They have a long, pink snout. Their favourite foods are earthworms and insects. They build a round nest of leaves and grass in their tunnel. Young are usually born during April and May. There are about three or four babies in a litter.

■ Moles

▼ *The velvety fur of a mole brushes in all directions. This helps them to run backwards quickly.*

Common shrew

Latin name: *Sorex araneus*

Habitat: woodland, hedgerows, thick grass

Body size: 55–82 mm, tail 22–44 mm

Weight: 5–12 g

Life span: up to 23 months

Shrews eat between 80 to 90 per cent of their body weight each day.

There are three main species of shrew living in Britain. The common shrew is the second most common mammal in the country. All three species of shrew have pointed snouts, small eyes, rounded ears and long whiskers. They also have short legs and short fur.

Common shrews have silky dark brown fur on their back. They have pale bellies with light brown sides. They dig for food such as slugs, spiders and beetles.

Common shrews build nests underground or under logs. Females have two litters a year.

Common shrews

▼ *Shrews are aggressive creatures. They live alone, except when they are bringing up their young.*

Pygmy shrew

Latin name: *Sorex minutus*

Habitat: woodland, hedgerows, thick grass

Body size: about 6 cm, tail 4 cm

Weight: about 4 g

Life span: up to 15 months

Pygmy shrews are the smallest mammals in Britain. They are smaller than the common shrew but have longer, thicker tails. They have medium brown fur with whitish bellies.

These tiny creatures need to eat every two hours or they may die. They eat insects, such as woodlice.

Babies are born from April to August. Nests are underground away from predators, such as owls and foxes. Many pygmy shrews get caught, but are not eaten because they taste horrible.

▼ *Pygmy shrews grow a thick coat of fur in autumn ready for winter.*

■ **Pygmy shrews**

Water shrew

Latin name: *Neomys fodiens*

Habitat: close to water, river banks, fenland

Body size: 67–96 mm, tail 45–77 mm

Weight: about 12–18 g

Life span: up to 19 months

Water shrews are the largest species of shrew in Britain. They are not seen as often as common shrews. Their velvety black backs with silver-grey bellies make them easy to spot. They nest in burrows or under logs near water. The nests are made from moss and leaves. On land they eat worms and insects. They hunt underwater for shrimp and small fish. The breeding season lasts from April to September. They can have up to three litters each year.

■ **Water shrews**

▲ *Water shrews can be vicious. Venom in their saliva stuns their prey.*

9

Pipistrelle bat

Latin name: *Pipistrellus pipistrellus*

Habitat: woodland, marshes, buildings

Body size: up to 45 mm, wingspan 20–25 mm

Weight: about 3–8 g

Life span: up to 16 years

Bats are the only mammal that can fly. They have two legs and two arms. The bones of their fingers are very long. These act as a frame for their wings.

▼ *Pipistrelle bats hunt for food before sunset.*

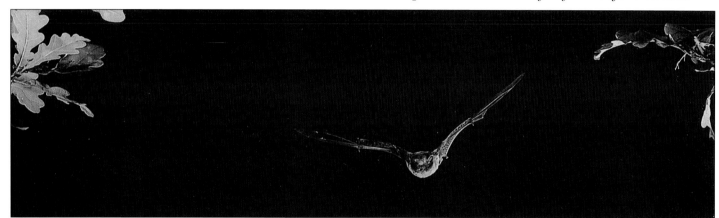

There are two species of pipistrelle bats. They are difficult to tell apart but scientists can identify them by their echolation calls. These are the high-pitched squeaks and clicks made by all bats. When the sounds reach an insect they bounce back sound waves. The bat uses these sound waves to find its prey.

Pipistrelles are the smallest and most common bat in Britain. They have dark red-brown fur on their backs. Their undersides are yellow brown. They have brown-black wings, noses and ears.

Pipistrelles fly about 5–10 metres above the ground. They move fast and twist and turn as they fly. These tiny creatures need to eat a lot of food. They can eat up to 3,000 insects a night. Bats roost in different places throughout the year. Trees and caves are their natural homes, but they can also live in buildings such as churches or even cellars. Young are born in June and July. Female bats usually have one baby in a year. In winter bats hibernate in warm places.

▲ *This bat is so small it could fit into a matchbox.*

■ **Pipistrelle bats**

Brown long-eared bat

Latin name: *Plecotus auritus*

Habitat: woodland, orchards, parkland

Body size: up to 45–50 mm, wingspan 24–28 cm

Weight: about 5–12 g

Life span: up to 30 years

Bat facts
There are 17 species of bat living in Britain. Many of these are rare. Two species are now 'vulnerable'. Another three are 'near threatened'.

Bats and their roosts are protected by law.

The second most common bat in Britain is the brown long-eared bat. They have brown fluffy fur on their bodies. They have pink-brown faces and grey-brown wings. Their ears are three-quarters the size of their body and head.

In the summer brown long-eared bats mostly live in woods. They fly close to trees, so they can be difficult to spot. Young are born in June. They hibernate in the winter.

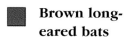 **Brown long-eared bats**

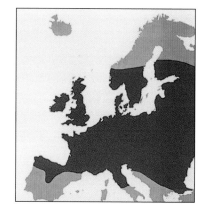

▼ *Brown long-eared bats have ears that fold away when they are resting.*

Daubenton's bat

Latin name: *Myotis daubentonii*

Habitat: trees, near water, under bridges

Body size: 5 cm, wingspan 25 cm

Weight: about 7–12 g

Life span: up to 22 years

Daubenton's bats fly close to the surface of water, catching insects. You may see them over lakes, rivers and canals shortly after sunset. They have a dark grey and brown furry body with a silver-grey underside. One of their most striking features is their large feet with hairy toes.

▼ *Daubenton's bats are also called 'water bats'.*

■ **Daubenton's bats**

In the past decade the number of bats has fallen. The biggest threat to bats is from people. We have destroyed many of the places that bats live. Farmers have sprayed insecticides on their crops. This kills the insects that bats like to eat.

Noctule bat

▲ *Noctule bats are sometimes called 'tree bats'. They like to roost in hollow trees.*

Latin name: *Nyctalus noctula*

Habitat: woodland

Body size: 6–8 cm, wingspan 32–45 cm

Weight: 19–40 g

Life span: up to 12 years

Noctule bats are among Britain's largest bats. Often they are the first bats to come out in early evening. They have sleek golden-brown fur. Their wings are long and narrow. They fly high in the sky and swoop fast to catch insects.

■ **Noctule bats**

Rabbit

Latin name: *Oryctolagus cuniculus*	
Habitat: dry areas with soft soil, fields, forests	
Body size: 38–50 cm long	
Weight: between 1.5–2.5 kg	
Life span: up to 9 years	

▲ *Farmers do not like rabbits because they eat their crops.*

 Rabbits

British rabbits in the wild mostly have soft, greyish-brown fur. Their undersides are pale grey and there is a flash of white fur on the underside of their tails. Rabbits have long ears and large eyes. They constantly listen and watch out for dangerous predators. Foxes, stoats and domestic cats are their biggest threat. If a rabbit senses danger, it thumps the ground with its back feet. This warns other rabbits to be careful.

Rabbits live in groups. They dig a network of burrows called a warren. You will often see holes in grassy areas that lead to the warren. Rabbits eat grasses, young leaves and shoots. They make their nests with grass, moss and fur from their bellies. Females give birth a few times each year. There can be up to 20 young in one litter.

> Rabbits are not native to Britain.
> Foreign invaders brought them
> to Britain about 900 years ago.
> The rabbits provided meat and fur.

Brown hare

Latin name: *Lepus europaeus*

Habitat: open grassland, farmland

Body size: 48–70 cm long, ear length 10 cm

Weight: 3–5 kg

Life span: up to 13 years

Brown hares are larger than rabbits. They are easy to tell apart from rabbits because hares have longer legs. They also have longer ears tipped with black. Their summer coats are brown but appear reddish-brown in winter.

Brown hares are usually found near open flat fields. They feed on herbs and wild grasses. Cereal and root crops are also tasty treats. Unlike rabbits, they do not make burrows. They mostly rest in hedgerows and woods during the day and come out at night. They breed all year round. Females can have up to three litters a year. Babies are called leverets.

Brown hares

▼ *Brown hares are the fastest mammals on land in Britain.*

Grey squirrel

Latin name: *Sciurus carolinensis*

Habitat: woodland, parks, gardens

Body size: up to 26 cm, tail up to 22 cm

Weight: 400–600 g

Life span: up to 9 years

Grey squirrels are not native to Britain. They were brought here from Canada and the USA in about 1870. In recent years black squirrels have started to appear in Britain. These squirrels are related to grey squirrels. They are aggressive and could wipe the grey squirrel out.

Grey squirrels have yellowish-brown fur in the summer months. In autumn, they moult their coats and appear silver-grey. They have large, bushy tails. Grey squirrels also have strong feet and sharp claws for climbing trees and walls.

The grey squirrel's front teeth grow all the time. They need to chew constantly to stop these teeth getting too long. Their diet includes nuts, seeds, tree bark, roots and flowers. In summer, squirrels build nests called dreys. Young are usually born in spring. Some mothers have a second litter in late summer. Grey squirrels do not hibernate. They store food for winter near their winter nests.

■ **Grey squirrels**

▼ *Grey squirrels spend a lot of time feeding on the ground. They have few predators.*

Red squirrel

Latin name: *Sciurus vulgaris*

Habitat: coniferous forests

Body size: 18–24 cm long, tail 18 cm

Weight: 250– 350 g

Life span: up to 7 years

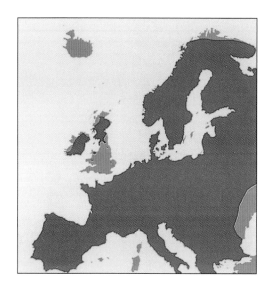

■ **Red squirrels**

▲ *Red squirrels are rarely seen on the ground. They leap from tree to tree.*

Red squirrels are native to Britain. Once they were common in England and Wales. Now they are only widespread in parts of Scotland. Larger grey squirrels have mostly replaced red squirrels in Britain.

In summer, red squirrels have reddish-brown fur. During winter, their fur is chocolate-brown with grey. They spend most of their time in trees. They eat nuts, berries and the cones from conifer trees. In late summer, they begin to store food under the soil for the winter. Red squirrels have fallen in numbers because grey squirrels are more successful in competing for food.

Red squirrels build nests or dreys close to the trunks of trees. They mate from December to September the following year. Females produce one or two litters a year.

Bank vole

Latin name: *Clethrionomys glareolus*	
Habitat: hedgerows, woodland, grassland	
Body size: about 8 cm, tail 6 cm	
Weight: 250–350 g	
Life span: up to 7 years	

▲ *Owls, weasels and foxes hunt for bank voles.*

■ **Bank voles**

Bank voles are widespread in Britain. They look similar to mice. You can spot the difference because they are chubby with round faces. They have blunt noses with small eyes and ears. Adult bank moles have long, shaggy red-brown fur on their backs. Youngsters have grey-brown fur. They all have creamy-beige undersides.

Bank voles live mostly in woods undercover of bushes and brambles. They eat buds, leaves, fruits and seeds. Sometimes they eat worms and insects. In autumn, they store food for the winter. During the winter, they will eat dry leaves. In summer, they build nests underground or in trees. They breed from March to October.

> **There are three species of vole in Britain. The bank vole is the smallest.**

Field vole

Latin name: *Microtus agrestis*

Habitat: long grass

Body size: 90–115 mm long, tail 40 mm

Weight: 20–40 g

Life span: about 12 months

There are about 80 million field voles in Britain. This means there are more field voles in Britain than human beings! They are not easy to spot, but they are easy to hear. They have loud squeaks and often make loud chattering noises.

Field voles are similar to bank voles but have greyish-brown fur. They live in long, rough grass. They eat mostly grass but also stems, bulbs and tree bark. They build grassy nests. Mothers often give birth to several litters in the summer.

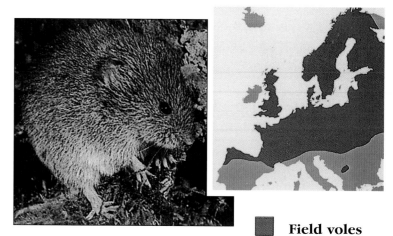

Field voles

▲ *Field voles make runways through rough grass.*

Water vole

Latin name: *Arvicola terrestris*

Habitat: banks of slow-moving rivers, streams

Body size: 12–20 cm long, tail 12 cm

Weight: 70–320 g

Life span: up to 2 years

Water voles are the largest of the British voles. They are often mistaken for water rats but they have rounder bodies, chubbier faces and shorter tails. Water voles have dark brown or black fur and fur on their tails.

Water voles live in burrows near riverbanks. Sometimes the entrance to their burrow is below the surface of the water. They are good swimmers. They eat grass and other plants. They can have up to five litters in the summer.

▲ *Water voles are falling in number. It is against the law to kill them.*

Water voles

Common rat

Latin name: *Rattus norvegicus*

Habitat: anywhere, especially near humans

Body size: 25 cm long, tail 22 cm

Weight: 200–400 g

Life span: up to 18 months

Common rats are not native to Britain. They probably came from China on ships about 250 years ago. Now they are the most common rat in Europe and most of North America.

Common rats have coarse grey-brown fur on their backs with pale grey bellies. They are often mistaken for water voles but they have pointed noses with bigger eyes and ears, and a longer tail.

Rats set up rat colonies near people. Large colonies are divided into small groups called clans. They dig networks of burrows and build nests underground. They can have up to five litters a year. There may be up to 14 babies in each litter.

Common rats are mostly active at night. They will eat anything from cereals, bones, crops and earthworms to human waste. They are considered pests because they can pass diseases to human beings.

■ **Common rats**

▼ *Common rats have an excellent sense of smell but they cannot see well.*

Wood mouse

Latin name: *Apodemus sylvaticus*

Habitat: woodland, grassland, gardens

Body size: 8–11 cm long, tail 9 cm

Weight: 16–27 g

Life span: up to 20 months

Wood mice are also known as long-tailed field mice. They have dark brown bodies with pale grey or white bellies. They have large ears and big black eyes.

Wood mice live in groups. They dig burrows and have nests underground. They breed all the time and can have six litters a year.

▲ *Wood mice eat seeds, nuts, buds and worms.*

 **Wood mice**

House mouse

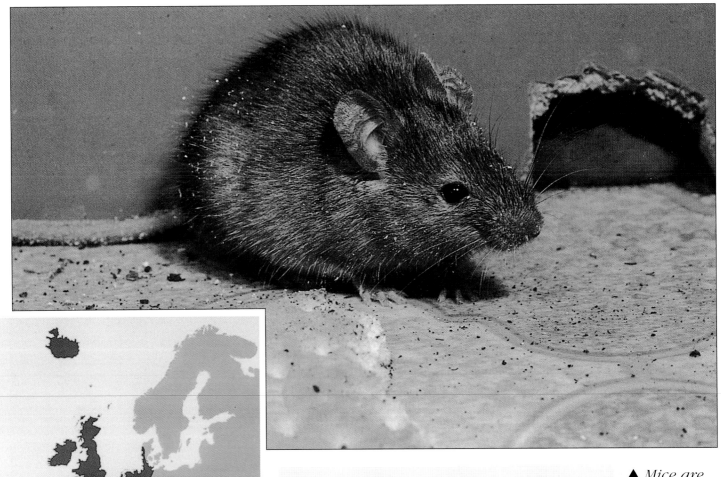

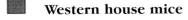
Western house mice

Eastern house mice

Latin name: *Mus musculus*
Habitat: buildings, open fields
Body size: 6.5–10 cm long, tail 8.5 cm
Weight: 12–22 g
Life span: up to 2 years

▲ *Mice are pests because they eat our food and carry diseases.*

House mice are not native to Britain. They started life in Asia but are now one of the most common mammals. They have grey-brown backs with paler bellies. They are similar to wood mice but have smaller eyes and ears, and shorter back feet.

These tiny creatures live in buildings. Often they make nests under the floorboards or behind skirting boards. They eat almost anything but prefer insects and cereal. A female can have up to 50 babies a year.

Harvest mouse

| Latin name: *Micromys minutus* |
| Habitat: reedbanks, hedgerows, long grass |
| Body size: 5–8 cm long, tail 6.5 cm |
| Weight: 5–11 g |
| Life span: up to 18 months |

Harvest mice are shy creatures, so they are difficult to spot. They have yellow-brown bodies with white bellies. Their tails are used for gripping as they climb.

These tiny creatures are active day and night. They eat seeds, fruits and sometimes insects. They build nests high up in stems of grass and plants. A female can have up to three litters a year.

■ **Harvest mice**

▲ *Harvest mice are the smallest species of mice in Britain.*

Dormouse

| Latin name: *Muscardinus avellanarius* |
| Habitat: deciduous woodland, hedgerows |
| Body size: 6.5–8 cm long, tail 6.5 cm |
| Weight: 15–30 g |
| Life span: up to 5 years |

The old English name for dormice is 'sleepers'. They spend nearly three-quarters of their life asleep and hibernate through the winter.

Adult dormice have bright, golden-brown coats. They have paler undersides and white throats. They also have long, furry tails. They spend most of the summer in trees. Their diet includes seeds, nuts, berries, flowers and insects. Females produce one or two litters a year.

▲ *Dormice are protected by law and cannot be killed.*

■ **Dormice**

Harbour porpoise

Latin name: *Phocoena phocoena*

Habitat: sea, usually within 10 km of land

Body size: 1.4–1.9 m

Weight: up to 55–65 kg

Life span: about 12 years

Harbour porpoises and bottlenose dolphins belong to a group of mammals called cetaceans. Cetaceans live in water. They hold their breath to dive. They return to the surface to breathe though a blowhole on the top of their head. Cetaceans are almost hairless. They have a thick layer of blubber below the skin to keep them warm.

Harbour porpoises are the smallest British cetacean. They are not easy to spot because they show little of their body above water. You may spot their triangular dorsal fin above the surface of the water. Most of their body is dark grey but they have paler patches on their sides and belly. They are chunky with small heads and no 'beak'.

Harbour porpoises live alone or in small groups. Their diet includes fish such as herring and mackerel, and squid and cuttlefish. Females usually give birth to one calf a year.

▼ *Harbour porpoises are a threatened species and protected by law.*

■ **Harbour porpoises**

Bottlenose dolphin

Latin name: *Tursiops truncatus*

Habitat: sea, estuaries, occasionally rivers

Body size: up to 3.8 m

Weight: up to 650 kg

Life span: unknown

■ **Bottlenose dolphins**

▼ *Bottlenose dolphins have sickle-shaped dorsal fins. This is another way to tell them apart from porpoises.*

You may spot dolphins anywhere in Britain. They are most common in the English Channel, Cardigan Bay and the Moray Firth Estuary. They are easier to spot than porpoises because they often leap out of the water.

Bottlenose dolphins have torpedo-shaped bodies. Their short snouts look like old-fashioned bottles. This is how they got their name. Dolphins vary in colour but are mostly brown or dark grey. They have light sides and white bellies.

These intelligent creatures eat mostly fish, squid and shrimp. They are social animals and usually live in groups. Sometimes they hunt for food together. They work as a team to herd fish together making them easier to catch.

Fox

Latin name: *Vulpes vulpes*

Habitat: woodland, open countryside, towns and cities

Body size: 50–90 cm, tail 30–50 cm

Weight: 6–10 kg

Life span: up to 7 years

▲ *About half a million foxes are born in Britain each year.*

> **Foxes are the most widespread and common meat-eating mammal in the world.**

The red fox is the most common species of fox. They are easy to recognise with their orange-red fur, bushy tails (also called a brush) and black feet. They have long, thin noses with white fur on their top lip. They are not much bigger than pet cats. They have excellent senses of smell, hearing and vision.

Foxes will live wherever there is cover and plenty of food. Many foxes live in towns and cities. They eat scraps from dustbins. In the countryside, they catch rabbits, mice, voles and wild birds in the summer. During autumn, they eat fruit, berries, insects and earthworms.

When foxes hunt, they stalk, then pounce on their victims.

You may spot a fox during the day but they are mostly active at night. The dog (male) and vixen (female) mate for life. They mate in December. At dusk, the male begins barking to attract the female. The female answers with a scream that sounds almost human. The female makes an underground den for her babies. She gives birth to around four or five cubs in March. The babies are born blind and deaf. The male brings food for the cubs. In autumn, the young move away to find territory of their own.

Foxes

▼ *In the winter, foxes grow thick coats of fur to keep warm.*

Stoat

Latin name:	*Mustela erminea*
Habitat:	woodland, farmland, marshes, mountains
Body size:	16–31 cm, tail 95 cm
Weight:	90–445 g
Life span:	up to 10 years

Stoats are common in Britain. They have long, slender bodies and short legs. Their short, black heads have long whiskers. Throughout the summer, they have ginger-brown backs with creamy undersides. They have a black tip on their tails. Stoats living in the north change colour in winter. They turn white, except for the tip of their tails. A stoat with a white winter coat is called an ermine.

Stoats have excellent senses of hearing and smell. They climb well and can run head-first down a tree. They are fierce hunters and will attack animals six times bigger than themselves. They eat small mammals, fish and reptiles. Stoats make their dens in hollow trees, rock crevices and empty rabbit burrows. They breed once a year. A typical litter may have between 5 and 12 kits (babies).

▲ *Stoats kill their prey with a bite to the neck.*

■ **Stoats**

▼ *A stoat with its white winter coat.*

28

Weasel

Latin name: *Mustela nivalis*

Habitat: woodland, farmland, grassland, sand dunes

Body size: 17–25 cm, tail 45 cm

Weight: 48–107 g

Life span: up to 3 years

▲ *Weasels can squeeze themselves down a mouse burrow.*

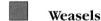 **Weasels**

Weasels and stoats look alike but weasels are smaller. Weasels have the same ginger-brown backs as stoats. However, they have white bellies and shorter tails with no black tip. This species of weasel is the smallest meat-eating mammal. Like stoats, they have good senses of hearing and smell. They also move quickly.

Weasels often build dens in burrows stolen from their prey. They are excellent hunters and kill their victims with a bite to the neck.

Their diet includes small mammals, birds and birds' eggs. They breed twice a year. They may have between four and six kits (babies) in a litter.

Mink

Latin name: *Mustela vison*

Habitat: near rivers, lakes

Body size: 30–40 cm, tail 17 cm

Weight: up to 1.5 kg

Life span: 2–5 years

▲ *Mink have a bad reputation because they kill animals even when they are not hungry.*

Mink

Mink are regularly spotted by day. They have chocolate-brown fur with slightly bushy tails. Their long, slim bodies mean they are good swimmers. They are also quick on land and can climb well. They don't see well but they have an excellent sense of smell. All these features make minks successful hunters. They eat fish, water vole, ducks, moorhen, rabbits, rats, birds and birds' eggs.

Adults have a few dens within their territory. Males will fight other males that come into their territory. Mink breed in February and the female gives birth to between five and six kittens.

Mink were brought from America in 1929. They were farmed for their fur. Many mink escaped or were released into the wild. The mink you see today are related to these animals.

Otter

Latin name: *Lutra lutra*

Habitat: rivers, streams, lakes, marshes, coastland

Body size: 55–110 cm, tail 45 cm

Weight: 5–12 kg

Life span: up to 10 years

Common otters are the only native otters in Britain. They are bigger than mink and have lighter fur. They are also better swimmers. They have webbed feet and powerful tails which they use to paddle through the water. When underwater, they close their ears and nostrils. They can hold their breath for up to three minutes. Their diet includes fish, crayfish, frogs and rabbits.

▼ *Otters are playful creatures. They slide around on muddy riverbanks.*

Otters always live near water but they are not easy to spot. They are most active at night. In the day they rest in dens called holts. These are usually underneath a pile of sticks or under tree roots. When they swim, only their heads show above the water. They breed all year and have between one to five young in a litter. In the 1950s the number of otters fell because of river pollution. In recent years the rivers have been cleaned up. Now the otters are returning to our rivers.

■ **Otters**

Badger

Latin name: *Meles meles*	
Habitat: woodland, open fields, hedgerows	
Body size: 80 cm, tail 15 cm	
Weight: up to 12 kg	
Life span: up to 14 years	

Badgers have black-and-white striped faces and stocky, silver-grey bodies. Their legs are short but they have powerful front paws for digging. They may be easy to recognise but they are difficult to spot. Badgers are shy and come out at night. Their sense of smell is around 800 times more powerful than our own. This means they can smell us and make a quick escape.

Badgers tend to live in areas of well-drained soil. This makes the soil easy to dig. They also need a good supply of food. They use their strong snouts to probe the ground for food. They eat insects, fruit, bluebell bulbs, young rabbits and hedgehogs. Their favourite snack is earthworms. These days, more badgers live in towns and cities. They will take scraps and food left out for them in gardens.

Badgers live in large family groups. They live in a network of tunnels called setts. A group may live in the same sett for hundreds of years. They line the sett with grass and leaves. Badgers are clean animals and clean their bedding regularly. They dig special dung pits away from the entrances to the sett. They also groom themselves and each other.

▲ *Badgers smack their lips noisily as they eat.*

> Each year about 50,000 badgers are killed on British roads. Many of these are following badger pathways made hundreds of years ago.

■ **Badgers**

Females give birth in February. They usually have one or two cubs. In April the cubs are big enough to leave the sett each evening. At this age they are very playful.

Badgers do not hibernate. If the weather is cold they stay underground. They live off the fat they have stored in the summer months.

▼ *Badgers mark themselves and their territory with a special scent.*

Common seal

Latin name: *Phoca vitulina*

Habitat: coast, fresh water

Body size: up to 1.9 m

Weight: up to 170 kg

Life span: females up to 35 years, males up to 25 years

Common seals or harbour seals are seen regularly around British coasts. They stay mostly within 20 km of the shoreline. At low tide you can spot them on rocks, mud flats and sandbanks. The hair of common seals can vary from black, to grey, to sandy-brown. They are usually speckled with dark spots. They have a more rounded head with a shorter jaw and mouth than grey seals.

Common seals dive well and can stay under water for long periods of time. They hunt fish and shellfish. They use their sensitive whiskers to track their prey and eat it whole.

Mating takes place in the water. Females give birth in June or July. They usually have one pup. Pups can swim and dive a few hours after they are born.

▲ *Common seals choose rocky spots to rest where they are safe from predators.*

Common seals

Grey seal

Latin name: *Halichoerus grypus*	
Habitat: rocky coastline	
Body size: up to 2.1 m	
Weight: up to 230 kg	
Life span: up to 40 years	

■ **Grey seals**

▲ *A grey seal rests on land. It can sleep at sea with its nose held out of the water.*

Inset: Grey seal pups have thick white fur. They put weight on quickly from drinking milk which is 60 per cent fat.

Over half of the world's population of grey seals are found in British waters. These seals are bigger than common seals. Males (bulls) are the largest mammals in Britain.

Grey seal hair varies from pale grey or brown with no spots to dark brown with large black splodges. Bulls are usually twice the size of females (cows). They feed on fish, especially cod and salmon.

Females give birth on rocks or deserted shorelines. They have a single baby (pup). Mothers stay with their pups for up to three weeks. When they return to the sea, the pups have to look after themselves.

Red deer

Latin name: *Cervus elaphus*

Habitat: deciduous woodland, moorland, mountains, open parkland

Body size: up to 1.2 m tall at shoulder

Weight: up to 225 kg

Life span: up to 25 years

The red deer is Britain's largest native land mammal. Deer that live in parks grow larger than those living in the mountains of Scotland. Red deer have reddish-brown coats. They also have a creamy patch on their rumps. In winter, their coats turn brownish-grey. Male deer (stags) have antlers. These antlers fall out each spring and grow again in August.

Red deer browse on deciduous trees, grasses, leaves and herbs. Stags use their antlers to fight each other. The strongest male wins a group of females (hinds) for mating. The mating season lasts from September to November. Females give birth in May or June. Usually, they have one calf.

■ **Red deer**

▲ *Male red deer have antlers shaped like branches. As deer grow older, their antlers become more branched.*

Fallow deer

Latin name: *Dama dama*

Habitat: deciduous woodland with open spaces

Body size: up to 1 m tall at shoulder

Weight: up to 30–50 kg

Life span: up to 16 years

Fallow deer

Fallow deer are not native to Britain, but are now the most widespread deer in the country. Their colour can vary but most have reddish-fawn fur with white spots in the summer.
They turn reddish-brown in the winter. They have a black line that runs along their backs to the end of their tails. Males (bucks) have flattened antlers.

Fallow deer eat grasses, berries, herbs and bark. Bucks and does (females) live in separate

▲ *Fallow deer fawns walk as soon as they are born.*

herds for most of the year. They only get together to mate. Females give birth to one baby (fawn) in June.

Roe deer

Latin name: *Capreolus capreolus*

Habitat: woodland with open spaces

Body size: up to 75 cm tall at shoulder

Weight: up to 18–29 kg

Life span: 10–12 years

▲ *Roe deer are usually seen in small family groups.*

Roe deer have short bodies with long legs. They also have short, white tails and white rumps. In summer, they have red-brown coats. By winter, their coats are grey-brown or black. They have white marks on each side of their nose and on their chins. Males grow small antlers in winter.

These small deer feed on buds and shoots of trees and grass. Females give birth in May and June. They are born with white spots on their fur.

Roe dear

Domesticated mammals

Domesticated mammals are wild animals that have been tamed by humans. These tamed animals are kept as livestock or pets. Long ago people began keeping animals to provide food and clothes.

Cattle

Wild cattle roamed Britain 2,500 years ago but these are now extinct. Today there are about 10 million domesticated cattle living in Britain. There are many different breeds. These are mostly used to provide milk or beef.

▲ *Jersey cows make rich creamy milk.*

Sheep

Domesticated sheep are descended from wild sheep. These wild sheep probably came from Asia thousands of years ago. Britain possibly has the largest selection of sheep in the world. These are kept for meat and wool.

◀ *This Suffolk sheep has a thick fleece of wool, good for a cold area with little rain.*

Pigs

Pigs are related to wild boar. Wild boar eat almost anything, so they were easy to domesticate. People kept them mostly for meat. There are many old breeds of pig in Britain. The best-known breed is the Large White.

▲ Pigs are very intelligent animals.

Horses and ponies

Exmoor ponies are the oldest wild ponies in Britain. Dartmoor and New Forest wild ponies are other old breeds. We know that people began domesticating horses over a thousand years ago. They kept horses for riding and to work on the land.

▲ Today, there are less than 5,000 wild Dartmoor ponies in Britain.

Pet and feral mammals

◄ *Pet cats can still act like wild animals. Especially when they hunt birds and mice.*

Cats

Domestic cats are probably related to Asian wild cats. The ancient Egyptians kept cats to hunt mice and rats. By the eighteenth century, people kept them as family pets. In recent years, cats have overtaken dogs as the most popular pet.

Dogs

Domestic dogs are related to wild wolves. Dogs were probably domesticated in ancient times. They were used for hunting and herding livestock. People still use dogs for working. However, they have become one of our favourite pets.

▲ *Dogs are often called 'man's best friend' because they make good companions.*

> People are also mammals! Like other animals, we have fur or hair on our bodies. Females give birth to babies. Babies can be fed on breast milk. However, humans walk upright on two legs. All other mammals walk on four legs.

Feral cats and wildcats

Animals that have escaped to live and breed in the wild are called 'feral'. In Britain, there are thousands of feral cats. They often live in small groups in empty buildings. They eat small mammals, birds and scraps.

True wildcats were widespread in Britain until the fifteenth century. However, they were hunted for fur and their forest homes were cut down. They nearly became extinct. Today a small number live in remote parts of Scotland.

▲ *The wildcat looks similar to a domesticated tabby cat.*

Small pet mammals

Small mammals called rodents make good pets, too. Guinea-pigs, gerbils, mice and rats are popular.

▼ *Small pets usually live in cages.*

Be a mammal detective

Look out for signs of mammals. Hunt for burrows, holes and nests, but do not disturb them. See if you can find animal tracks. Watch out for nuts or cones that have been eaten away. You can also look for animal droppings.

Mammal tracks

On soft ground or after snow you may be lucky enough to find mammal tracks. Keep a record of the tracks you find. Note the date and place you discovered them. Draw the tracks of front feet and back feet.

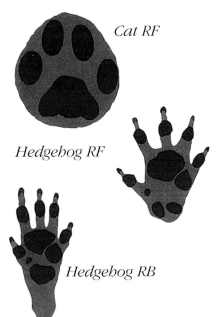

Cat RF

Hedgehog RF

Hedgehog RB

Badger RF

Badger RB

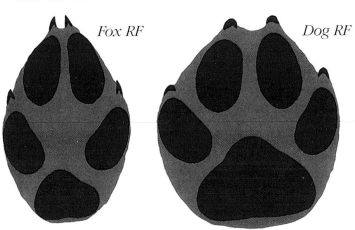

Fox RF

Dog RF

These tracks are life-size. RF means that the tracks were made by the mammal's right front foot. RB means the right back foot.

Plaster casts

You could build up a collection of mammal footprints by making plaster casts. To make a plaster cast you will need:

a strip of card about 5 cm wide
paper clips
a 500 g margarine tub
plaster of Paris
a tablespoon
water
a stick or spoon for stirring
newspaper
a trowel

1   Clear away any grass or leaves around the track.

2   Take the strip of card and fix the ends together with a paper clip. You will now have a circle of card. Place this over the print.

3   Add 5 heaped tablespoons of plaster with water in the margarine tub. Mix until it is like smooth cream.

4   Pour the mixture into the circle of card. Let the plaster set for 30 minutes.

5   Lift out the cast and card. At home, clean and label the cast.

Droppings

Be on the lookout for mammal droppings. These are often left to mark a mammal's territory. Make a note of the size, colour and hardness of the droppings.

These droppings are all life-size.

Common rat

Pipistrelle bat

Wood mouse

House mouse

Field vole

Rabbit

Hedgehog

Fox

Badger

Food clues

You can sometimes tell the mammals that have been in a place by the chewed food left behind. Many mammals enjoy hazelnuts. You may be able to tell which animal has been eating a nut by the marks left on its shell.

Dormouse (right)
A smooth inner rim. Tooth marks at an angle on the outer surface.

Wood mouse (left)
Parallel marks on the inner rim. Rough marks on the outer surface.

Bank vole (right)
Parallel marks on the inner rim. No marks on the outer surface.

Squirrel
Left: Shells cracked open. Jagged edges on soft, unripe clusters.

Right: Hardened nuts prised apart.

Spruce cone eaten by wood mouse

Spruce cone eaten by squirrel

43

Making homes for mammals

A hedgehog shelter

Hedgehogs sometimes visit gardens in summer for food and shelter. In winter, they need a safe place to hibernate. If you have hedgehogs in your garden you could make a special house for them.

Build the house with wood that has not been treated with any chemicals. Cover your house with a sheet of heavy polythene. Cover this with soil and leaves. Make sure the ventilation tube is not covered. Do not disturb hedgehogs when they are hibernating.

Bat boxes

You could make bat boxes and fix them high up on trees. You will need wood that has not been treated with chemicals. It should be at least 25 mm thick.

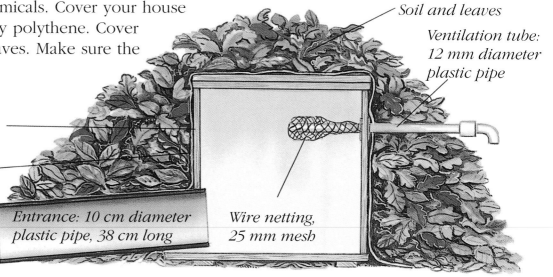

Soil and leaves

Ventilation tube: 12 mm diameter plastic pipe

Wooden box: about 30 x 30 x 30 cm

Polythene sheet

Entrance: 10 cm diameter plastic pipe, 38 cm long

Wire netting, 25 mm mesh

Ask an adult to help you build boxes and food tables.

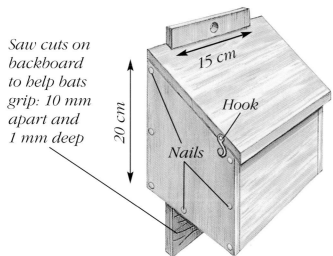

Saw cuts on backboard to help bats grip: 10 mm apart and 1 mm deep

15 cm

20 cm

Hook

Nails

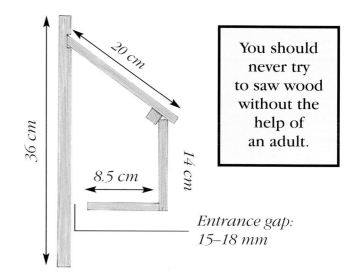

20 cm

36 cm

8.5 cm

14 cm

Entrance gap: 15–18 mm

You should never try to saw wood without the help of an adult.

The entrance to the box should be 15–18 mm wide. Do not make it any bigger. Place the box in a sunny place. Do not disturb the bats in the box.

Mammal watching

There are many ways to watch mammals without disturbing them.

Plants for bats

Grow plants that have a strong scent at night. The scent will attract insects that bats eat. Dusk is the best time to watch bats feeding.

Make a food table

You could build a food table for voles and mice (as shown, right). Use branches to make pathways to the table. Protect the table with chicken wire.

Put food on the table just before dusk. Raisins, seeds, nuts and fruit are good. In the morning, look for food remains and animal droppings.

Food table

Hide and see

Make a special hiding place or 'hide' to watch mammals. You could make your hide from an old blanket. Put the blanket over a clothes-horse or poles of wood.

Warm summer evenings are best for watching mammals. Wear dark clothes. Cover your torch with red see-through plastic. This helps you to see the animals without them being able to see you. Get in your hide before dusk. Stay still and quiet. Make notes of everything you see.

Mammal behaviour

Watch kittens and puppies play. Chasing, pouncing and shaking toys are similar to hunting for prey.

Watch cats rubbing up against people, walls and furniture. They are marking their territory.

Watch human beings, too! Look how parents protect their children.

▶ *Mammals often smell you before they see you. Remember to keep your distance!*

Glossary

Aggressive Fierce and threatening behaviour.

Amphibian An animal that lives on land but breeds in water. Frogs and newts are amphibians.

Colony A group of animals of one species living close together.

Coniferous forest A forest with evergreen trees such as pines and firs. These trees do not shed their leaves.

Crops Plants, such as wheat and barley, that are grown by farmers.

Deciduous woodland A wood with trees such as oak and ash. These trees shed their leaves in autumn.

Domesticate To tame an animal to live with humans as a pet or livestock.

Dorsal fin The fin on the back of a sea mammal.

Echolocation A way of finding objects, usually food, using sound.

Extinct Describes a species of animal that no longer lives.

Habitat The place where a plant or animal lives in the wild.

Hibernate To spend winter sleeping.

Insecticide Strong chemicals that are sprayed on plants to kill insects.

Litter A group of babies born at the same time to one mother.

Mammary gland The gland in female mammals which makes milk.

Marine To do with the sea.

Moult To loose hair, fur or feathers so a new coat or feathers can grow.

Native Belonging to a place or country.

Nocturnal Awake at night.

Polluted Made dirty, sometimes by chemicals.

Predator An animal that hunts and kills other animals for food.

Prey An animal that is hunted and killed by another animal for food.

Reptile An animal with scaly skin that is cold-blooded and lays eggs. Lizards, snakes and crocodiles are reptiles.

Roost A place where birds or bats rest.

Species A group of animals or plants that are similar.

Territory An area that an animal or group of animals claim as their own. They mark the territory with scent. They will fight other animals to keep them off their territory.

▲ *Magpies picking insects from the coat of a red deer.*

Further information

Books to read:

Amazing Life Cycles: Mammals
Honor Head (Ticktock Media, 2007)

British Wildlife: Foxes Sally Morgan
(Franklin Watts, 2005)

Bubblefacts: Amazing Mammals
(Miles Kelly Publishing, 2004)

Classifying Animals: Mammals
Sarah Wilkes (Wayland, 2007)

Mammal-watcher's code

- Never go out alone, especially at night.
- Always tell someone exactly where you are going and how long you expect to be.
- Always ask permission before going on private land, and tell the owner what you found.
- The animals come first: avoid disturbing them.
- Respect the habitat you are exploring.
- Don't drop any litter or damage plants.
- Close gates and keep to the edge of crop fields.

Find out more about the marvellous world of mammals

The Mammal Society
3 The Carronades, New Road,
Southampton
SO14 0AA
Email: enquiries@mammal.org.uk
Website: http://www.abdn.ac.uk/mammal/

The Bat Conservation Trust
15 Cloisters House, 8 Battersea Park Road,
London SW8 4BG
You can even join the Young Batworker's Club. Check the website for more details.
Website: http://www.bats.org.uk/

The Badger Trust
PO Box 708, East Grinstead RH19 2WN
Website: http://www.badger.org.uk

Whale and Dolphin Conservation Society
Brookfield House, 38 St Paul Street,
Chippenham, Wiltshire SN15 1LJ
Website: http://www.wdcs.org.uk/

Index

Page numbers in **bold** indicate pictures.